Dr. Ruth Talks About Grandparents

Dr. Ruth Talks About Grandparents

ADVICE FOR KIDS ON MAKING

THE MOST OF A SPECIAL RELATIONSHIP

Dr. Ruth K. Westheimer with Pierre A. Lehu

Pictures by Tracey Campbell Pearson

Farrar Straus Giroux ■ New York

ACKNOWLEDGMENTS

Some family members, friends, and colleagues who were instrumental in their support of my work must be mentioned: Pierre and Joanne Lehu, Marga and Bill Kunreuther, Fred Rosenberg, Bonnie Kaye, Martin Englisher, and Steven Kaplan. Also, I would like to thank our editor, Beverly Reingold, our copy editor, Karla Reganold, and Abby Sider, editorial assistant. —R.K.W.

The four people who gave me the most insight into what being a grandparent is all about were the grandparents of my own children—my parents, Pierre and Annette Lehu, and my in-laws, Joseph and Anita Seminara. And although my family is small, I learned a lot about how a large family operates from that of my wife, including her sister, Juliette, brothers Joseph and Frank, and their spouses, Tony, Cecelia, and Mariah; her grandmothers, Antonietta and Mary; her Aunt Jo and Uncle Paul; and all the other uncles, aunts, cousins, nieces, and nephews, whose warmth and love have been a blessing to share. But most of all I have to thank the person who manages to make me laugh at least once a day, Ruth K. Westheimer, not only for agreeing to work with me on this book but also for allowing me to share in the thrill of the sixteen-year rocket-ship ride that has been the making of the legend of Dr. Ruth. —P.A.L.

Library of Congress Cataloging-in-Publication Data
Westheimer, Ruth K. (Ruth Karola), date–
   Dr. Ruth talks about grandparents : advice for kids on making the most of a special relationship / Ruth Westheimer ; with Pierre Lehu ; pictures by Tracey Campbell Pearson.
     p.   cm.
   Summary: Advises readers to treasure their grandparents and suggests ways in which they might enhance their relationships.
   1. Grandparents—Juvenile literature.   [1. Grandparents.]   I. Lehu, Pierre. II. Pearson, Tracey Campbell, ill. III. Title.
   HQ759.9.W384   1997
   306.874'5—dc21   96-45197

I dedicate this book to the memory
of my beloved parents and grandparents,
who in an indescribable sacrifice sent me,
their only child and grandchild, to safety, and who
perished in concentration camps during World War II.
Their set of values, joie de vivre, and
positive outlook live on in me and in my family:
Fred Westheimer, Miriam Westheimer,
Joel Einleger, Ari and Leora Einleger, Joel Westheimer,
and Barbara Leckie.
—R.K.W.

To the grandparents I never knew, to my great-aunt and great-uncle, who
took over the role when I was growing up,
to my parents, who gave me more than enough love to make up
for not having grandparents, to my wife, Joanne,
and to my children, Peter and Gabrielle.
—P.A.L.

Generations come and generations go,
but the earth remains forever.
Ecclesiastes I:4

Contents

Dr. Ruth Talks About Grandparents

. . . grandparents love you . . .

Foreword

Ari calls me Omi. Ari is my grandson, and I asked my daughter, Miriam, to have him call me Omi because that's what I called my grandmother when I was a child living in Germany. Omi isn't the official word for grandmother in German—that's *Grossmutter*—but it's an affectionate name that many children in that country call their grandmothers. Ari calls my husband Opa, though the real German term is *Grossvater*. And both of us are waiting until our grand-daughter, Leora, is old enough to use those terms also.

If you were to ask children around the world what they call their grandparents, you'd find that in most cultures there's a special nick-name for them. In France it's Mémé and Pépé. In Spanish-speaking countries it's often Abuelita and Abuelito. In Yiddish it's Bobbe and Zeyde. In Italian it's Nonna and Nonno. In Greek it's Yiayia and Papou. And in America it might be Grandma and Grandpa, or maybe Granny and Gramps.

I think it's wonderful that children have special names for their grandparents, because the relationship between grandparents and their grandchildren is a very special one. It's so special that I wanted to write a book about it.

What is it about grandparents that sets them apart? They love you. I know, lots of people love you. But grandparents love you in a way that no one else in the world does. I know how much the love of my mother's parents (who lived on a farm) meant to me, as well as that of my father's mother (who lived with us; my father's father died before I was born). And the feeling I have for my little Ari and Leora can be so strong that it's almost like a hurt, but a good hurt, if you know what I mean.

Unfortunately, even the best relationships don't come easily. Love is like a plant: it grows bigger and stronger if you give it plenty of sunlight and water; it dies if you neglect it. My goal in this book is to teach you how to make the love between you and your grandparents not only live but flourish.

What kinds of things are you going to find out? Well, did you know that inside every single grandparent there's a boy or girl just like you? Because the body gets older doesn't mean that the spirit gets older too. The more years you spend on this earth, the more you learn, but even though you grow smarter and more mature than you were as a kid, there's still a child inside you. Grandparents still like to have fun. They still enjoy playing tricks on people. Or making them feel good. And very often it is by being with and playing with their grandchildren that grandparents are able to express the child inside.

Now, that little child is also inside your mom and dad, but they don't always let it show. One reason is that they're very busy; it takes a lot of work to raise children and make money and keep a house or apartment neat and clean. The other reason you don't always see that little child in your parents is that they try to hide it. Since they have to make sure that you always obey them, they may not want you to think of them as friends. Oh, they play around with you from time to time, but they also have to make sure that you do your homework, straighten up your room, and take out the garbage. After all, raising you is their duty.

Your parents' supervision naturally causes conflicts between you and them. So does their seeing you as a child even while they want you to grow up and become an adult. They worry about you and feel a tremendous sense of responsibility. You, on the other hand, just want to grow up. You want to feel independent, and you can't if you're always hanging on to Mom and Dad. So while you owe everything you have to your parents, you're also trying to separate yourself from them. The process isn't easy, and it can lead to feelings of guilt on both sides, and conflicts that at the time appear quite intense.

But unless your grandparents are actually raising you, those conflicts don't usually form part of the relationship. There are no power struggles, because they don't have the primary responsibility for how you turn out, and you don't have to break away from them to achieve independence. The relationship between you and your grandparents is sort of like a demilitarized zone, a place where you can all let your hair down. You may act silly with them, in a way that you wouldn't in front of your parents, and they don't mind if you get to look behind their wrinkles and gray hair and see that little kid who is still in there. That's one reason they like to show you old pictures of themselves, so that you'll see them when they were younger and realize that they weren't always old.

And here's another surprise for you. Inside you there's a part of your grandparents. When you look at them, to some degree you're also looking at yourself. So while you're learning about your grandparents, you're going to find that you're also learning about yourself.

1

Grandparents Through the Ages

Whatever the relationship you have with your grandparents, when you hear the word grandma or grandpa, your mind probably conjures up an image of a cuddly older man or woman. This picture, more or less accurate today, is a fairly recent one in history. If you were to travel back in time, you would find that grandparents weren't always quite so warm and affectionate, especially grandfathers.

While your grandparents probably don't live in the same house or apartment that you do, that's not the way it used to be, and in many countries, like China or India or various nations in Africa, that's not the way it is today. The so-called nuclear family, a family composed of only two parents and their children, is a recent development. What was far more common throughout history was to have three or even four generations, from babies to their great-grandparents, all living together under one roof, often in one large room. Imagine yourself in that situation, living with ten or twenty other relatives in your grandparents' house, and right away you can see how much different your relationship with your grandparents would be. There would be a lot more of you sharing their attention, and if they got on your nerves, you wouldn't be able to go to your room and turn on the stereo.

But it wasn't just the living arrangements that were different, it was also the family structure. Most early societies were called patriarchies, which means that the eldest male, the patriarch, was the head of the household and what he said was absolute law. If you've ever studied the Bible, then you know that Abraham and Moses were patriarchs in the society of the early Hebrews. The ancient Greek and Roman societies were also patriarchies, and this system is still in force today, especially in countries that remain basically agricultural, such as India or Ethiopia.

Suppose you lived three thousand years ago in the land of the Hebrews, where the majority of people lived and worked on farms. At that time the most important asset your family could own was land. If your father or grandfather was still alive and owned the land you lived on, you had to obey him because if he threw you out of the house, you would have almost nowhere to turn. If you were left on your own, probably the only way you could support yourself would be to work on somebody else's farm, and that other landowner would pay you very little money in exchange for a lot of hard work. So you see, much of a patriarch's power came from his owning the family farm.

. . . all living together under one roof . . .

In addition to the financial hold that the patriarch had on his family, there were also religious reasons why he was looked up to by those younger than himself. Among the early Hebrews, God was called "the Ancient of ancients," and the Bible told its followers to "honor the aged." In those days people didn't live as long as they do today, and so to reach an advanced age, which meant old enough for your hair to turn gray, was a major achievement for which you were given respect by everyone else in the tribe or village. Also, because an older person is closer to death, people believed that he or she was closer to God. Even pagan societies, where people didn't believe in one god, respected the elderly for their proximity to their ancestors.

Another reason the elders were important in prehistoric times is that in a culture where writing is unknown, the whole history of the tribe survives through the stories that are handed down from generation to generation. The elders of the village know the old stories best and so are a critical link to the past. Also, when information is scarce and there are no books or newspapers, people are very concerned about maintaining their connections to the past, which, if lost, can never be regained.

Even though the patriarch was the absolute ruler of his family, he was dependent on his sons and grandsons. Agriculture is labor-intensive. In a time when there were no tractors or combines, as a man grew older and weaker he had to rely on the strong arms and legs of his sons and grandsons. There was no government system like Social Security to support the elderly. If a man wasn't able to grow his own food, or if he didn't have a family to do it for him, he would probably starve. Male children and grandchildren were considered valuable assets, sort of like an early retirement account.

And since many children died young from one disease or another, a man had as many children as possible, hoping that enough would survive into adulthood to help sustain him and his wife, or more likely a few wives, in their old age.

Naturally, relationships between our early ancestors and their grandchildren were nothing like ours. Once a child reached the age of four or five, he had to behave respectfully toward his grandparents, especially toward his grandfather. In many societies, a child couldn't even sit down in front of his or her grandfather without asking permission. And the grandfather didn't ask his grandchildren to do things, he ordered them.

Remember, you wouldn't have been able to run home to Mom and Dad, since you all would have been living under one roof. Also, even as a small child you would have realized already that your parents, too, had to jump when Grandfather gave them an order. So while children may have loved their grandfathers way back then, they were probably a bit afraid of them as well.

By the way, in case you picture this grandfather as a very old man, let me remind you that people didn't live as long as they do today. Just a hundred years ago, only 37 percent of men and 42 percent of women lived to the age of sixty-five. And if you were a fifteen-year-old in 1900, you would have had only a one in fifty chance of still having all four of your grandparents around, as compared to today's odds of one in six. Go farther back in time, and men or women in their forties were considered to have lived a long time. That doesn't mean that all people died in their forties, just that there were far fewer people in their sixties and seventies than there are today.

With so many people living together under one roof, there had to be firm rules to keep order in the household. Since the house belonged to the grandparents, they would demand, and receive, compliance. You know that you listen to your grandma and grandpa more readily when you're at their house than when they visit you, right? So if you lived in their house permanently, you would have to respect their wishes more.

Now, my guess is that grandmothers, even way back in Biblical times, had a soft spot in their hearts for their grandchildren and would put up with a lot more than their husbands. Certainly they spent more time with the children than the men did. But because women had many more children in those days, there was a good chance that a grandmother might still be raising some young children of her own when she had grandchildren sitting at her feet. While she may have wanted to spoil her grandchildren, she might not have had the time.

Why has the relationship between grandparents and grandchildren changed so much? Why is it that instead of being afraid of your grandfather you can't wait to see him? One important reason, especially in the United States, is migration.

There have been two types of mass migrations in America. The first involved the people who came to these shores from Europe, Africa, and Asia. The second involved people who moved from the Eastern states to the Western frontier. Since younger people tend to emigrate while older ones remain behind, suddenly tens of thousands of children not only weren't living in the same house as their grandparents but were moving hundreds or maybe thousands of miles away from them.

If you were a child who'd crossed the ocean to come to Amer-

. . . there had to be firm rules . . .

ica, or crossed the Great Plains to live on a farm or ranch on the frontier, you would be totally out of your grandparents' control. Living that way, you wouldn't expect to have that kind of control over your own grandchildren. So because of these shifts in the way people lived, the whole concept of grandparenting underwent some very big changes.

Another reason for the changing relationship between grandparents and grandchildren was the Industrial Revolution. As goods began to be mass-produced in factories instead of made at home, more and more people left the family farm to work in cities, where they had much smaller living quarters. Grandparents might still live nearby, but they weren't in the same house with their families. Back on the farm, machinery began to replace laborers, so even those who remained in agriculture lived in smaller families.

It may surprise you to learn that a further reason that the farming families grew smaller was the signing of the Constitution, which affected more than merely the structure of our government. Just as the forces of democracy set aside the powers of the king, they also began to erode the power of the patriarch. In a monarchy, when the head of a family died, his assets were passed on as a whole to his eldest son, who succeeded him as the patriarch. Under new sets of laws passed by both national and state legislatures in the United States, the family property was more likely to be divided equally among all the children, so that the eldest son no longer dominated.

Finally, demographic changes altered the way we view older people. As advances in medicine allowed men and women to live longer, senior citizens began to multiply. Once they were no longer rarities, the younger generations didn't automatically grant them the respect they once did, and so even grandparents became a little less special to their grandchildren.

Recently I witnessed a dramatic change in the status of some grandparents. I wrote a book about the 1991 airlift of several thousand Ethiopian Jews to Israel. Those people traveled not only hundreds of miles but nearly hundreds of years as well, going from a tribal civilization to a modern one. To highlight the change I witnessed, I put two pictures on the jacket of the book. One was taken when the Ethiopians first landed, and in it everyone was in traditional dress, with the grandparents in the forefront, clearly the heads of their families. The other picture, taken only a few months later, showed the grandchildren, now sporting jeans and sneakers, in front and the grandparents all the way in the back. For this set of grandparents, the world had really been turned upside down.

Today the relationships between grandparents and grandchildren vary greatly, and seldom, at least in America, are they based on the patriarchal model of old. Having been a grandchild many years ago, and being a grandmother now, I certainly notice the difference in the relationship I had with my grandmother and how my grandchildren and I interact, and in my opinion, the changes have been all for the good.

2

What Is a Grandparent?

Why do adults think all kids are alike? Why do they assume that you're going to drop that container of milk, dirty the rug with your muddy feet, or make a lot of noise? Why can't they see that every kid is as much an individual as every adult?

I'm sure you don't like being treated as if you were just a kid. But let me ask you another question: do you ever look at old people and think of them as being all the same? It's true that many of them have gray hair. Many walk a bit slower than they used to. Many may not hear as well as they once did. Most of them tell stories about things that happened a long time ago. But are all old people the same? Does their having problems associated with growing older make them less worthy in some way?

In England, a group of researchers disguised themselves as older people to see how they would be treated. They discovered that many young people consider old people a nuisance. They talk down to them, treating them as if they were little children. And instead of trying to help them, they avoid them.

What is your impression of older people? While sometimes they may appear all alike to you, deep inside you know they're not because of what you know about your grandparents. They are certainly unique, right? You appreciate their individual ways. Maybe it's the foreign nickname that your grandmother calls you. Or that your grandfather always seems to be wearing a sweater, even when it's sweltering outside. You don't even think of them as old people, they're just your grandparents. But you should also remember that the vast majority of old people are grandparents, too, each one unique and special to the people who love him or her.

Grandparents come in many different packages. Some are old and frail, while many are on the young side, with plenty of energy. Some are retired, but many still go to work every day or do all the chores that it takes to run a house. Some grandparents live nearby, while others live far away. Some grandparents are couples, sometimes newly remarried, while others are widows and widowers. And some have passed away, perhaps before you were even born. But there is one thing all grandparents have in common: they were the mothers and fathers of your own mom and dad. And this has a direct effect on you, even if you've never met them.

Whether or not you think you look like any of your grandparents, you definitely share with them some very important ingredients called genes. Genes are the codes that make you you. They are the instructions that determine the shape of your nose, the color

. . . many still go to work every day . . .

of your eyes, how tall you are going to become, and every single other detail about you. You got these genes from your parents, who got their genes from *their* parents, your grandparents. Since these genes get mixed together, you never look exactly like either of your parents, and you don't look exactly like your grandparents either. Still, all the genes that made *you* originally came from your grand-parents.

Imagine taking four picture puzzles, dumping out the boxes on the floor to make one big pile out of all the pieces, and then mixing them up. Then imagine taking one quarter of those pieces and putting them together to make a new picture. Now pretend that they fit together. You wouldn't get the same picture as in any of the four puzzles, would you? Of course not. But you would be able to recognize the individual pieces from each of the other four puzzles.

You are that imaginary puzzle, made up of the different pieces that came from your four grandparents, and if you look closely at yourself, you'll recognize some of the pieces that come from them. I certainly know which gene I got from my grandparents, the one for shortness. I am only four feet seven inches tall, and the reason I never grew beyond that is not that I was a picky eater as a child, which I was, or that I ate too many sweets, which I did, but that all four of my grandparents were short.

You don't need to have your grandparents in the room to make this comparison. All you need are some pictures. And the older those pictures are—meaning the younger your grandparents are in the pictures—the easier it will be to see the resemblances. Try this the next time you can get ahold of some family albums.

You are that imaginary puzzle . . .

But looking at pictures or even examining your grandparents in the flesh won't tell you the whole story, because some of what you share with your grandparents isn't visible. I'm not talking about the shape of your heart or thigh bone or stomach, although if one of your grandparents has a large stomach you may want to start doing sit-ups now. No, what I'm talking about is your intelligence and your personality.

If one of your grandparents was very good at playing a musical instrument, then there's a chance that you are, too. If one of your grandparents had a nasty temper, then maybe that's why you get grumpy for the slightest reason sometimes. And if three or all four of your grandparents were very good at making friends, then the chances are that you, too, have that ability.

I know of another gene that I got from a grandparent, and that's the gene for talking. My parents would sit in a room all evening, barely saying a word, so I certainly didn't become a nonstop talker because of them. My grandmother Selma, however, would sit and talk with me for hours. I'm sure we share the gene that kept our mouths going.

Of course, genes don't absolutely control your life. Let's say you have the gene for friendliness, but you happen to be an only child raised on a farm where your nearest neighbors are several miles away. In such circumstances, you might not be able to exercise your ability to be friendly, so that now when you meet new people, you may think of yourself as being shy. This is where knowing about your background can come in handy. If it's likely that deep inside you there's a built-in tendency to be friendly, then you're not really shy at all. All you have to do is practice being outgoing, and you'll probably be able to change that bashful aspect of your personality in a flash.

So you see, the more you learn about your grandparents—what it was like growing up when they did, where and how they lived, what they dreamed of, and what their children, including your parents, were like—the more you're actually learning about yourself. For that reason alone, you might want to know as much as possible about your grandparents.

Another reason to explore your grandparents' past with them is that they have actually lived through periods of history that you have only heard about, and may not *even* have heard about, but probably will have to study one day in school. While books can certainly convey what a particular time period was like, you can get a much clearer picture from real people, especially people you love. I know it was because I told my daughter about my experiences as a young girl in Israel that she went there to live for a time. If your grandparents tell you stories about the places where they lived, I'm sure you'll want to visit those countries or cities.

You should know that your grandparents have witnessed tremendous changes. When they were your age, life was far different from what it is today. Think of all the modern conveniences you consider necessities that didn't exist for your grandparents. It might help you appreciate your grandparents' early lives, and I'm sure it will make you more grateful for some of the items you take for granted, such as microwaves and computers.

Besides telling you about changes, your grandparents can provide you with an anchor to the past by sharing the many aspects of life that have remained the same. They can tell you about holidays, which they probably celebrated much the way you do. They can tell you about all the ways in which their moms and dads took care of them, just as yours take care of you. They can give you examples of many of the freedoms of our society, which have helped to keep this country strong over the years, such as voting and going to church or synagogue.

In recounting their history to you, your grandparents will be telling you about the childhoods of some very important people— your parents. Right now, your parents are the closest people you have in the whole world. Yes, you can learn about them by look- ing at pictures of them as children, but you can learn even more by asking their parents what they were like at your age. Probably you'll find that your parents' experiences were similar to your own. They played sports, they got hurt, they had problems at school. Maybe they've told you some of those stories, but you'll notice that your grandparents have a different perspective. They may even differ on the details, but that's all right. You're not writing a history book, you just want a picture of what life was like for your parents when they were growing up, which may help you to figure out why they're the way they are today—and why you're the way you are.

Before long, these stories that you hear about your grandpar- ents and your parents are going to become your stories. As you grow older and have your own children and grandchildren, you're going to pass on these stories. And you may not only tell the stories, you may also add how and when you first heard them. So in addition to their genes, grandparents pass on to you their entire personal his- tory, which will become part of your history as well.

One problem with trying to get information from your grandparents might be that they have a habit of telling the same story again and again. A long time ago, before there were books, repeating old stories was the only way to pass on information, and many of the stories in the Old Testament were told from generation to generation before being written down. But today you might think that hearing the same story over and over again is boring, like having to watch a TV show you've already seen.

Well, aren't there some shows you love so much that you're willing to watch them again and again? The episodes of *I Love Lucy* were probably filmed forty years ago, but many people get great enjoyment from watching Lucy perform her antics on reruns. And if there's a song that you particularly like, do you tire of listening to it, or of watching the music video, after only one or two times? Or if you get a new video game for your birthday, do you play it only once and put it away forever? Of course not, because repetition isn't necessarily a bad thing.

But let's say that there's a story Grandma is about to begin that you've heard a few too many times. It can happen, even to the best of stories and the best of storytellers. Or maybe you wouldn't mind hearing it another time, but just not today. What should you do? You could say something like, "Grandma, that's a great story, but I've got to go do my homework (or wash the car, or clean my room, or whatever). I'd love to hear it again another time, though." Grandparents know that sometimes they go on and on and need to be reminded not to, but it's important that the reminding be done with respect.

Now, there are ways in which you could make such storytelling more interesting for yourself, especially when you've heard the story a thousand times. One is to ask questions. When Grandma launches into the story of the time Uncle Lou got his car stuck in the mud, stop her and ask whether Uncle Lou was married. Then she'll probably tell you about his wife and start another story—if you're lucky, one that you haven't heard. Sometimes grandparents are trying to tell you not a particular story but, rather, any story from their past. They can't always be sure whether you've heard the one they're telling, and they don't mind a little guidance. If you can steer them into a new one, or at least one that hasn't been repeated too often, they'll be happy, and you'll find yourself more interested as well. And since they have a whole lifetime of stories, you probably haven't heard them all.

Another way of making such storytelling more enjoyable is to throw in some related stories of your own. If Grandpa is talking about the time he went fishing with his brothers along the Mississippi River, and you've got a good fishing story, don't be afraid to put your two cents in. Grandparents love to hear—and to pass on— new stories.

Besides an extensive personal history, grandparents have acquired a lot of knowledge over the years, whether or not they got degrees in school, and they'll gladly share as much of it as you want. Sometimes you need help with homework or an idea for a science project. Or maybe you need more practical knowledge, such as the best polish for shining your shoes, how to tie a lure on a fishing line, how to hit a baseball, or how to make a delicious pot of soup.

Mom or Dad might be able to help you, too, but they might also be very busy. A great thing about grandparents is that they usually have the time and inclination to answer questions. They'll proba-

. . . how to make a delicious pot of soup.

bly do it with so much enthusiasm that you'll feel even more eager to learn. They can be what are called mentors, people who don't just provide information but who also give you guidance and perhaps inspiration.

Don't let geographical distance from your grandparents stop you. If they live far away, call to ask them your questions. If you think the call will cost too much, ask your grandparents to call you right back and pick up the cost. I bet you they'll be glad to.

Of course it's easier when you can talk face-to-face with your grandparents. I remember when my friend Susan was in sixth grade and her class was told to write a report on an assigned country. Susan got Italy, and, boy, was she glad. Both of her grandparents had been born in Italy, and she knew that she'd be able to get lots of information from them. That night she called her grandma and made an appointment to visit on Saturday morning.

Her grandparents lived in a town ten miles away, but her grandpa was happy to drive over and pick her up. Susan spent the entire morning learning about her grandparents' homeland and afterward was served her favorite lunch—spaghetti and meatballs.

There is no escaping that the older you get, the closer you are to dying. No one wants to leave this earth, except perhaps people who are suffering terribly from illness, but the passing on is a whole lot easier if you know that you've left behind a part of yourself. For a grandparent to pass on to a grandchild some of what he or she has learned in life is a very meaningful process. It makes having lived to a certain age worthwhile. So as you're listening and learning, keep in mind that you're also making your grandparents feel very, very good.

3

When Grandparents Live Nearby

It's really great to have grandparents living nearby. When I was a little girl, my parents shared an apartment in Germany with my grandmother, so she was as close as possible, and for me that was fabulous. But your grandparents don't have to live that close to be considered nearby grandparents. As long as the proximity is such that you can see them regularly—let's say at least once a week—they qualify.

If you have grandparents who live nearby *and* those who live far away, then you know that you have a different relationship with each set. You naturally become closer to the ones you see all the time. There are no awkward silences, because you have lots to talk about. I'm sure you've discovered that it's easier to communicate with someone you know well than with someone you haven't seen in a long time. There is so much to say to the person you haven't seen for a while, too many gaps to fill in, that you don't know where to begin. But when you see somebody often, the conversation you have with that person seems like a continuation of the one you were having when you last left each other.

On the other hand, if you're not a natural-born talker like me, it's possible that even if you do see your grandparents all the time, you have little to say to them. This can happen with the best grandparents. But to avoid such awkwardness, all you need is a little planning.

I know that on a normal, day-to-day basis, you and your grandparents may not seem to have much in common. You're busy with school and friends, and they have different activities, such as card playing or gardening. You like different music, different TV shows, different books and magazines. So if you're going to have fun together, you have to pick out ahead of time some activities that you'll both enjoy.

Is there a favorite dish of yours that Grandma makes? If so, there's a good chance that this dish is of foreign origin, because so many of our families started out in other countries. If Grandma's background is Hungarian, maybe she makes great goulash. Or if she's Irish, maybe it's her soda bread that you love. Whatever the dish, it would be a good idea to learn how to make it so that later you'll be able to make it for yourself, your kids, and your grandkids. Just be sure to let your grandma know ahead of time that you want her to teach you how to cook that special dish, so that she'll have everything she needs, as well as the time to work with you.

I know a girl named Danielle who always looks forward to seeing her grandmother because her grandmother is teaching her how to knit. When Danielle was about five, her grandmother let her help prepare the wool, which came in long bunches. Her grandmother would stretch the wool across Danielle's arms while quickly twirling it into a ball. When Danielle was eight, her grandmother taught her some simple stitches, and now that she's eleven, they're making a sweater together.

Interestingly, Danielle's mother cannot knit a stitch, even though *her* mother is teaching Danielle. Danielle's grandmother had four kids, so there never seemed to be enough time for her to teach Danielle's mother how to knit. But now that she is a grandmother, she really enjoys teaching Danielle, and Danielle is getting great satisfaction from watching the sweater take shape.

Another fun activity to share with grandparents is looking at old pictures. Sometimes even Mom and Dad forget which relative is which, especially if the pictures are really old. But Grandma and Grandpa will be able to tell you who's who, and you might want to write down the names on the back of the pictures. Probably while you go through these old pictures, your grandparents will tell you some good stories, and by the end of the session all of you will be exhausted from laughing.

If you really want to get the names of all your family members straight, why not spend an afternoon making up a family tree. With your parents' permission, you might consider cutting faces from old pictures and gluing them to the names.

No matter how often you've heard your grandparents' stories, when you most want to remember them—let's say, when you're telling your children about their family history—you might find

. . . teaching her how to knit.

that you've forgotten important details. So it might be a good idea to make an official record of these stories by taping them. You can use a simple tape recorder, but if you have access to a video recorder, you might want to make videotapes of your grandma and grandpa telling the stories. The tapes will be fun to play whenever you get together with the rest of your family—aunts, uncles, and cousins—at family gatherings and holidays such as Thanksgiving, Hanukkah, or Christmas.

Since talking into a tape recorder can be tiring, don't try to record these stories all at once. Make a tape every once in a while. Just make sure that you write down which stories your grandparents have already told on tape so that you don't have the tale of Uncle Lou stuck in the mud ten times.

If you want to make some of those old stories really come to life, go back and visit the old neighborhood where they happened. That won't be possible if your family has moved very far away, but if they haven't, it would be fun to see the house or the barnyard or the alley where a famous incident in your family's history took place.

Traveling with grandparents can be fun even if you don't have a family-related place as a goal. The trip doesn't have to be long, or even to someplace special. There may be a bowling alley twenty miles away that you've never gone to, and an afternoon spent driving and bowling with your grandparents might be more amusing than sitting in their living room. During school vacations, maybe they could take you someplace farther, where you'd have to spend a few nights at a hotel. A nearby big city would provide lots of things to do and see. If you live in the city, then a trip to the country might be just the thing.

To make the most of an opportunity to travel with your grandparents, schedule trip-planning as part of the fun. Deciding where to go can be almost as pleasurable as actually going there. When you've chosen your destination, buy a map and determine ahead of time exactly what it is you want to see and explore. If you're going to a place lots of people like to visit, I'm sure you can find information about it in a library book or on the Internet. The more you know about a new place, the more you'll enjoy your visit there, and your grandparents can help you find out what you should know.

This reminds me of my young friend James. James was studying American history in his fifth-grade class, and one evening he was discussing some of what he had learned with his grandfather. His grandfather asked him if he had ever visited Williamsburg, Virginia. He hadn't, and he didn't know why his grandpa was asking him. Then his grandfather explained to him that Williamsburg is a city that has been restored to look the way it did during the time of the American Revolution. People dress up in period clothing and perform activities of the era, such as making horseshoes and candles. Williamsburg sounded like a great place to visit, and two weeks later his grandparents took James and his younger brother there for a weekend trip. The two boys had a great time, and by seeing what America was really like back then, James found his American history lessons a lot more interesting.

If you're thinking about a summer trip with your grandparents and you don't have a particular place you want to visit, how about going to camp? There actually is a grandparents/grandchildren camp in the Adirondack Mountains, where you and one or more of your grandparents can spend a few weeks going on nature walks, taking canoe trips, and just sitting around the campfire roasting marshmallows.

But even if you can't leave home to go somewhere exciting with a grandparent, you can take an imaginary trip that will almost be like the real thing. You can have the fun of picking the place, just the way you would if you were going there. You can still study a map, you can still read all about it. Then all you have to do is rent a travel video of the place and watch it together. Afterward you can share a meal of the native food and pretend that you're there. If you choose Beijing, then you can have Chinese food. If you choose Rome, you can have pasta. If Paris, then gorge yourself on French fries. You get the idea.

If you see your grandparents regularly, you can make a habit out of "going" someplace new each month. Then you can buy a big map of the world and stick little pins in each country or city that you've "visited." You'll have a great time, and you'll learn a lot of fascinating geography.

What's great about imaginary trips is that you don't have to limit yourself to different places; you can also go back in time. This might be especially fun if the trip involves an event your grandparents once experienced. Let's say there was a big world's fair that they visited, or maybe a country where your grandfather's army division served during a war. Or there was a record snowstorm in the area where one or both of them lived. You can look up any of those times and places and then pretend that you were there with them. Your grandparents will make great guides.

Your grandparents should also make great teachers, and they may want to teach you things that will require a little more effort

. . . take an imaginary trip . . .

on your part, effort that you feel isn't worth your time and energy. For example, if you like rock music and they love opera, you might resist the idea of sitting down with them to listen to one of their favorite operas. Or if they speak another language, you might say to yourself, I get enough homework from my teachers, do I really have to learn their language just to please them?

Well, from a purely practical point of view, the information they are trying to give you is worth quite a lot. If you decide later on that you want to learn the language of your ancestors—or any language for that matter—and hire a private tutor, it will probably cost you fifty dollars an hour, and here are your grandparents offering to do it for nothing. (I speak four languages, and I wish I knew even more.) Besides, you might actually enjoy learning a new language—or listening to opera.

You should also keep in mind that your grandparents will immensely enjoy being able to pass on to you something from their culture. I know that between school, homework, and after-school activities, you don't have a lot of free time. But I also know that if you're open to learning from your grandparents, you'll all benefit enormously from the exchange.

Even if your grandparents don't wish to teach you something in particular, I'm sure they do plenty for you. Take it from me, grandparents are the most unselfish people in the world when it comes to their grandchildren. If your parents aren't careful, your grandparents might really spoil you. (Just ask my daughter about my grandchildren, Ari and Leora!) But while grandparents love to give to their grandchildren, and grandchildren love to receive, the relationship between grandparents and grandchildren is much stronger when it's a two-way street.

. . . listening to opera.

Are you saying to yourself, But I don't have any money, so what can I give them? Not having money for gifts is a problem faced by all children, especially on birthdays and holidays. However, you shouldn't worry about this, because all your family members know that your "job" is going to school, and since you don't get paid for doing that, they realize that you can't afford to buy costly presents. I can guarantee you that adult members of your family, especially grandparents, will be absolutely delighted if you remember to mark the occasion by making them something.

You see, there is one thing that you do have to give and that's your time. If you make a card, the recipient knows it took time and will appreciate it. If you shop for a key chain or a paperweight or some other inexpensive gift, the time you spend and the thought you give it matter most.

But do you know what the very best gifts are? They're the unexpected ones people get, when it's not a holiday or a birthday. And they don't have to cost a penny. What kind of gifts am I talking about? Mostly help. If your grandparents live in a house nearby, you can lend a hand in many ways. You can cut the grass, shovel the walk, put up or take down the storm windows, set the table for Sunday dinner and even help cook it, vacuum, wash windows, clean out the garage, brush the cobwebs from the attic, or hang up the wash. The older your grandparents are, the more assistance they need with chores that require physical effort, and I'm sure they would really appreciate receiving yours.

If your grandparents live in an apartment, you might help them do the shopping, especially carrying their packages up stairs. You might pitch in to clean the apartment. You might bring up the mail

. . . shovel the walk . . .

for them. Wherever they live, you might rearrange their closets in the spring and fall, putting away one set of clothes and bringing out another. You might go to the post office to buy them stamps. You might return their empty bottles to the supermarket or go to the dry cleaner for them.

And you wouldn't be doing these chores strictly for your grandparents. The other beneficiaries would be your parents. They would certainly like to be more helpful to your grandparents, who are their parents, after all. But they may have trouble finding time to do their own chores, so popping over to lend a hand to your grandparents might be very difficult. If you help them out, your parents will be pleased because their child is acting responsibly, and they'll feel less guilty about your grandparents.

A grandparent who is a widow or widower living alone could use another gift, and that's your touch. All people need to be touched, and people who live alone rarely get enough touching. If you simply take their hand or give them a hug, you will be surprised how much they appreciate it.

Here's a gift idea that I'll bet you never thought of. You know all those magazines and comic books that you buy? Pass them on to your grandparents! Sounds crazy, right? I know they would never buy them on their own. But let's say you really like rock music and you regularly read a rock magazine. If you give your old copies to your grandparents, maybe they will take a look at them. Then when you go over to visit, they might ask you questions about some of the articles, and maybe even agree to listen to some of the music they read about. They might even like it! At the very least, reading magazines aimed at kids will help your grandparents understand you better. But be prepared: you might wind up with the hippest grandparents on the block!

"Over the river and through the woods to grandmother's house we go" is the beginning of a holiday song with which I'm sure you're familiar. But even if Grandma and Grandpa live right next door, or downstairs or upstairs, you have to remember one thing: their house is not your house.

Actually, your house is not your house either, because whether it's a house or an apartment, it belongs to your parents and they make the rules. But since you live with them full-time, they're more used to bending those rules in your favor. And if you have your own room, they will even respect your privacy to some degree. They may let you decide how to decorate it, or at least let you put up some posters of your favorite singers or actors, and if you've closed the door, they should know to knock before coming in.

But while your grandparents are the closest relatives you have besides your parents and siblings, and while you may feel very comfortable at their house, especially if you visit quite often, you should still keep in mind that the rules are different there.

Why is it important that you obey those rules? The best reason is that it keeps you close to your grandparents. If they're always worried that you're going to misbehave in their house, then your relationship won't be as good as it would be if they felt they could trust you.

Trust is a key word in any relationship. Certainly it's vital to have trust between yourself and your parents. If your mom can't trust you to behave at home while she goes to the store, then her only choice is to take you with her—even if your favorite show is on TV, you have a lot of homework to do, or you're expecting a call from your best friend. By the same token, if your mom says that you can go out and join the other kids in a ball game at a certain hour, then she shouldn't suddenly change her mind without a good reason. You simply have to be able to count on each other.

You should be able to count on your grandparents, too, to be so close that you can talk about almost anything, including things that you might not want to share with your parents. Consider the case of my friend Geoffrey, who lived in a big city. One of his closest friends, Paul, lived on the same block, and from the time they were old enough to play out on the street, they were always together. When they started junior high, Paul went to a different school, and a few months later, Geoffrey discovered that Paul was into smoking marijuana. They still would see each other and throw a football around, and Paul kept asking Geoffrey to try the drug, which Geoffrey wanted no part of.

Geoffrey had thought of going to his parents with his dilemma, but he was afraid they would insist that he stop seeing Paul, which would make Geoffrey look like a wimp to all of his other friends on the block. Worse, since Geoffrey's parents were friends of Paul's parents, they might go to them, making Geoffrey a rat. Because Geoffrey wanted to get the advice of an adult, he went to his grandfather, who lived a few blocks away.

Geoffrey asked his grandfather to promise that he wouldn't tell his mom and dad anything that he was about to reveal. Since he knew he could rely on his grandfather's promise, he then told him the whole story.

Geoffrey's grandfather knew that if Geoffrey said he wasn't going to try marijuana, he could trust him, and he also had an idea about what Geoffrey could do to help his friend. His grandfather asked him if any of the other kids on the block had gone along with Paul and tried marijuana. When Geoffrey said they hadn't, his grandfather suggested that they all get together and promise one another to stay away from drugs and to try to stop Paul.

Geoffrey felt really relieved after speaking to his grandfather. He had been able to discuss the whole situation, and his grandfather had given him some great advice about helping his friend.

Because Geoffrey and his grandfather could trust each other, Geoffrey was able to solve his problem. His issue was a pretty serious one, but grandparents can help you out in all sorts of ways, both big and small. Of course, how much help they can provide depends on how close you are to them, and how close you are depends, at least in part, on how you act around them.

Now, if every time you go to your grandparents' house, you just head for the den and plop down in front of the TV, barely saying hi as you pass, do you think you're going to have a close relationship with your grandparents? Or if you act like a slob at the dinner table, will they trust you to water their plants while they're away? You may not make that connection, but you can be sure they do. Picture the conversation. Grandpa suggests to Grandma that they ask you to water their plants. Grandma says to Grandpa, "But you know how Jimmy is, he'll make a mess and spill water all over the place, just the way he does when he eats." Grandpa will shake his head and say, "I suppose you're right, dear." And they won't ask you.

If you were a fly on the wall and heard that conversation, I bet you would be disappointed. I know you would want to be entrusted with watering the plants, that it would make you feel good to do it. That's why you have to stop and consider your actions around your grandparents, even if they love you to death no matter what you do.

If you've been out playing all morning, should you put on a clean shirt before going over to visit your grandparents? Should you remove the headphones to your Walkman when you pass through the door to greet them? If you burp at the dinner table by accident, should you say excuse me? If you're asked a question such as "Do you like school?" should you give a one-word yup or nope, or should you take the time and energy to give a good answer, maybe tell about your favorite subject? If you pull out the old photo albums, should you leave them lying around or put them back where you found them? If you're given a snack in the living room, should you just leave the plate on the floor or take it back to the kitchen?

These may seem like little things, but they do add up. Remember, your grandparents probably don't see you every day. How you act when you're around them determines their impression of you. And you should show them that you love and care enough for them to consider your behavior when you're together.

What if you do see your grandparents daily? Or maybe you even live with them? Does that change anything? The answer is yes and no. Obviously you shouldn't have to be on your best behavior every single moment, especially when you're in the place you call home. You have to be able to let your hair down, as the saying goes, at some point. So if you live with grandparents, or if one of them lives in your parents' home, then your relationship is going to be somewhat different—but only somewhat.

You see, grandparents come from another era. They have a different lifestyle, and there has to be some compromising if everyone is going to live in peace. It is just as important for them to be comfortable at home as it is for you, even if that home is also your home.

Music is often an issue that splits the generations. While your parents may have grown up listening to rock, it's doubtful that your grandparents like it. And at issue here is not only the style of music, but the volume at which it is played. Before all instruments were electrified and amplified, music couldn't be played as loud as it is today. So although you may enjoy your CDs the most when the volume is turned way up, it's definitely going to make any grandparents in the vicinity miserable.

And let's say that you're in the habit of studying while lying on the couch looking down at your book, which is face up on the floor. Your grandmother is going to take one look at you and tell you to sit correctly or you'll get a headache. Now, perhaps you've been doing this for years and never gotten a headache, and you get straight A's to boot. Still, your grandmother is going to get upset.

Am I going to tell you never to play loud music or study with your head hanging off the couch? No, just compromise a little.

As far as the music is concerned, you should go to your parents, explain the situation, and ask them to buy you the best set of headphones they can afford. That way you won't have to listen to your music through tinny little earphones, but can enjoy it to the fullest extent even when your grandfather is around. And when he's not around, then you can unplug yourself.

While music carries throughout the house, your grandma has

... *studying while lying on the couch* ...

to be in the room to see you doing your imitation of a bat study-ing history. If you're aware that she's nearby, why not just go to your room and hang off the end of your bed. And when she's not around, you can resume your perch on the couch.

You may think it unfair that suddenly you have to make changes because of a grandparent. But it's not a question of fairness. It's just that for this world to continue, for there not to be constant battles, people have to do things for one another, even some things they don't want to do.

The truth is, the more you fight it, the worse it will be. If you just say, Okay, I'll try to make Grandma or Grandpa happy, then pretty soon you'll develop new habits that you'll like and that won't upset them. But if you decide that it's going to make you miserable to make these adjustments, then you will be miserable.

Did I ever tell you about William? William's grandmother lived upstairs in the house that he shared with his parents. Since his parents both worked, his grandmother often had to watch him, which was fine with William, except that sometimes she took his mother's instructions too literally.

One summer afternoon, William grabbed his baseball glove and got ready to meet his friends at a nearby park. But William had been sick, and his mother had told his grandmother that he wasn't sup-posed to leave the house. So as William walked out the door, his grandmother followed him, telling him that he had to go back home. He ignored her, and when he got to the ball field, he started playing right away. As long as he was on the field, his grandmother stood about ten feet away, all the while telling him that he had to go home. One of his friends yelled out, "If she's gonna stay there, why don't you give her a glove." At that point, William gave up and led his grandmother back home.

William had thought that he could disobey his grandmother, who was following his mother's instructions, after all. But it didn't work. Even though he hadn't listened to her, she'd found a way to shame him into obeying her. Isn't it too bad that she had to do that?

You know, when I was a little girl I lived with my parents and my grandmother. I loved my grandmother, but sometimes she annoyed me. She was so overprotective that more than once, when all my friends were playing in a nearby park, she kept me from going. I cried and shouted, but still she would not let me go. Then, when I was ten, I was separated from my parents and grandmother during the war, and later I became an orphan. I'm sixty-nine now, and there are days when I still regret the times I upset my grandmother. So think before you behave disrespectfully, and there will be peace not only among your family, but also within yourself.

4

When Grandparents Live Far Away

There's no doubt that if your grandparents live far away, your relationship is going to be a lot different than if they live nearby. It's not just because they're your grandparents; you'd feel different about *anyone* who lived far away. If you've ever had a best friend who moved away, then you probably know what happens. You swear that you'll always be best friends, you promise to stay in touch and see each other as often as possible, but after a while you drift further and further apart. You make new friends, you stop missing your old friend as much, and in many cases you wind up never seeing each other again.

Grandparents aren't like friends, since you can't just replace them. And while you may never see your friend again, I'm sure you'll keep seeing your grandparents. But when you do see them, whether they come to your house or you go to theirs, even though they're your grandparents you're going to feel a little awkward around them for a while.

This feeling is natural. You might think that you'd have so much more to say to someone you haven't seen in a while, but when faced with six months' or a year's worth of your life to tell about, you end up saying little or nothing. In response to your grand-mother's question "How's school?" you can't tell her about every test, every class, every friend, so you might give her a one-word answer, "Fine." It's not that you don't want to tell her, it's just that there's so much to say, you don't know how to get started.

Don't worry about it. Just because you're tongue-tied when your grandparents first walk through the door doesn't mean that you won't find the words later on. Most likely, the farther away your grandparents live, the longer you'll be together during your visits. In time you'll get comfortable—after all, they're not strangers but your grandparents—and you might find yourself telling them all about what's been going on in your life since you last saw them.

Whatever you do, don't give up on talking with them. Don't de-cide that since you're not sure what to say, you'd rather go out and be with your friends. You can always be with your friends, and you'll probably regret the lost opportunity to spend this special time with your grandparents. And remember that if you've been doing a good job of communicating with them all along, then starting a conversation will be a lot easier.

While you can't help faraway grandparents the way you can nearby ones, the best thing you can do for them is maintain good communications between them and your whole family. Luckily for you, you live in an era when keeping in touch has never been easier. Just imagine that you lived during the time of the Pilgrims and your family had moved from England to America while your grandparents stayed behind. In those days it took ships three months to cross the ocean, and they didn't go back and forth all that often. Under those circumstances, you'd be lucky if you could exchange one set of letters a year. Today, with telephones, fax machines, computers, audiotapes and videotapes, and, yes, overnight mail, you can always stay in touch.

Now, I spend hours every day on the phone, so no one can say that I'm not a big fan of telephones. But when it comes to communicating with your grandparents, I don't think the phone is the best way. Why? Your grandparents are going to ask you how you are, and you're going to be tempted to say "Fine" and leave it at that. While you're on the phone, especially on a long-distance call that you know is costing a lot of money, you won't be able to think of all the interesting things that happened to you since you last spoke to your grandparents.

I suppose you could try to prepare for your phone call. You could write down what it was you wanted to say, sort of like a script. But would you really do that? And what if your grandparents called when you weren't ready? No, I don't think the phone is always the best way to communicate. It's important that you talk to your grandparents on the phone. It's good that they hear your voice and hear you say that you love them. But don't make the phone the only link between you and your grandparents—be sure to write, too.

"But I'm not a good writer," you say. My reply is that your grandparents care not *how* you write but *what* you write. They won't

. . . be sure to write . . .

mind if there are some spelling errors. It won't bother them if your handwriting isn't great, as long as they can read it. They won't care if the letter is short or long, on paper with lines or without, with ink blots, eraser marks, or Wite-Out all over it. They'll love getting your letters, just as long as the letters convey how you're really doing.

And then you've probably heard the old saying, practice makes perfect. It will certainly apply to your letters: after a while, writing them will become much less difficult. What's more, as your writing improves, you'll find it easier to do your homework and take a test. Writing well is very important in life, and here's a chance for you to learn while you're giving a lot of happiness to people you love.

My suggestion is that you not plan on writing a long letter. The letter could become a chore that you keep putting off. I think it would be better if you wrote a little bit to your grandparents every day. That way the events of the day would be fresh in your memory. Then, at the end of the week, you could stick the pages in an envelope and mail them off.

By the way, you might want to consider these letters a record of your life, a sort of diary, but one you're willing to share. If you write on loose-leaf paper, just ask your grandparents to return the letters after they've read them. Then you can put them in a binder and you'll have it, a diary. Incidentally, if there are parts of your life that you don't feel like sharing, write about them on separate sheets of paper and put these directly into your notebook. That's the advantage of using a loose-leaf binder: you can move pages around.

If you don't like the idea of hand-writing a diary, and you're able to communicate with your grandparents via computer, you can still keep a record of your letters. All you have to do is keep a copy of all the letters you write in a special file. These copies will serve the same purpose as a diary, and I know you'll enjoy reading them later on. And if you don't want your little brother getting ahold of them, instead of saving your letters on the computer's hard drive, put them on a separate disk that you can keep locked in your room.

Although you'll certainly have fun writing and later rereading those letters, the people who will enjoy them most are your grandparents. No doubt they'll talk about what you said, not only with each other but also with the neighbors, which may be especially important if your grandparents are slowing down and don't have many stories to pass on about their own activities. One funny incident from your life might end up entertaining dozens of people in a city far from your home.

I want you to understand the importance of your stories so that you will put in as much detail as possible. Think of your letters as paint-by-number pictures. If you fill in some of the numbers and leave the others blank, someone looking at that picture might be able to tell what it is but won't find the image clear and affecting. The same thing will happen with your letters. The more you fill in that painting in your grandparents' minds, the clearer the image they'll get of your life. So it's actually better to tell them a lot about one or two experiences you had than very little about many.

When I was a ten-year-old living in Germany, I was sent to a school in Switzerland to get away from the Nazis. My parents and my grandmother had to stay behind. For several years we were able to exchange letters. But because the Nazis would read those letters, we couldn't say as much as we would have liked to. When my grandmother wrote to me, she couldn't really complain about the conditions, because she might have been punished. The Nazis eventually did kill my parents and my grandmother. I still have all the letters they sent, and I treasure them dearly, even though they are more than fifty years old; I only wish that they contained more details. But there are no censors looking over your shoulder when you write, so include as much information as you can.

Whether or not you have news to report, you can always write to your grandparents. You could write them a poem or a short story. You could tell them about a dream you had. You could list your baseball-card collection or your best friends in school and tell why you like them. You could put together a family scrapbook, with tests that you did well on, a Thanksgiving dinner menu that you made up, and a list of the family's favorite TV shows, all accompanied by photos that you took. Don't wait to finish it, but mail them a page or two at a time. They can put it together at their end, and when you go to visit, your whole family can share in the fun.

My grandson makes me pictures, and I have them hanging all over my apartment. One reason is that they remind me of him. Another is that I want him to know how much I appreciate his making them for me. You see, even though he is the one making the pictures, we're both using them to communicate how much we love each other.

Of course, you should keep in touch with your grandparents any way you can, using any or all of the modern tools of communication. Maybe you could volunteer to maintain the ties between your family and your grandparents. You could keep a record of when you or other family members call and remind them when it's time to call again. If, let's say, your little sister didn't get to talk to your grandparents the last time because the phone call was placed after her bedtime, you could remind your parents that this time the call should be made when she's available.

Another way to keep in touch is by recording messages on a cassette and mailing it to them. These messages don't necessarily have to be reports of what you're doing. If you play a musical instrument, you could send your grandparents a concert on tape. Or if you have younger brothers or sisters who can't write, you could work at getting them to put messages on tape. Even *googoo gaga* will sound great to a grandparent.

If your family has a camcorder, you can easily show your grandparents what's happening in your family life. Certainly making a tape for them during important events such as birthdays and holidays is appropriate, but you might find it amusing to make tapes of everyday occurrences, too. Some potential subject matter might include: a typical morning as everyone is getting ready for work and school, the family at lunch or dinner, Dad working on some project in his workroom, or your brother learning to ride his bike.

My advice is to not make any one video too long, or it will get boring. Just make little vignettes, slices of your family's life, then send off the tape when you have half an hour's worth or so. Keep in mind that videotape can be used again, so if there's nothing special on a particular tape, such as an important birthday party, ask your grandparents to send it back to you. By reusing it, you'll help protect the environment.

Besides keeping in touch with your grandparents, there are

other ways to maintain closeness between them and your family. If physical disabilities, such as cataracts or arthritis, make it difficult for your grandparents to write to people, you could volunteer to address their Christmas cards for them, or make a newsletter about what they're doing and send it to your aunts, uncles, and cousins.

If your grandparents have a particular interest, a hobby such as stamp collecting or gardening, or if they're suffering from a disease, such as diabetes, you could collect information about it and send it to them.

Do you ever make decorations for your house on the holidays? How about making some extras for your grandparents so that they can decorate their windows with your artwork?

If your grandparents have a favorite sports team whose games they can no longer see because they've moved away from the area, you could tape the games and send the tapes to them.

If your grandparents used to live in your neighborhood, you could cut out articles from the newspaper about community events for them. Or you could even play reporter and document these changes yourself. Say a new building went up, you could take pictures and send copies to your grandparents. You could call up some of their old friends and neighbors and ask them how they're doing and then write up what they said.

You could play board games with your grandparents by mail, fax, E-mail, or phone. Chess is probably the best game, because you can use the time between moves to ponder your strategy, but even Monopoly would work. For non-strategy games you might need to set up only one board, which I think should be at your grandparents because it will make them feel good to see it. And, by the way,

... some extras for your grandparents ...

you don't have to be the only grandchild playing. Brothers, sisters, and even cousins could join in.

You and your grandparents could arrange to read the same book. Then, on the phone, you could talk about what was happening in the story and the parts you liked best.

You could read through the comics and pick out your favorite ones, then mail them so that you can laugh together.

If you're good at sewing, you could make a quilt with your grandmother, each sewing squares separately and maybe putting them together when you see each other.

If you know that one of your grandparents is a fan of a particular actor, actress, singer, or sports hero, you could write to the individual and ask for an autographed picture. Have it sent to your house and then give it to your grandparents.

If you have grandparents who came from another country, they might enjoy reading books written in their native tongue. These are usually expensive if bought new, but if you scour every yard sale, thrift shop, and book sale, you're bound to locate one or two used copies that you could send to them or give them when you next see them.

But you know, you don't have to do things that affect your grandparents directly to make them feel good. You can always help other people in their name. If one of your grandparents is suffering from a disease—cancer, for example—you could collect empty bottles, deliver groceries or newspapers, or mow lawns to make money. Then you could give this money to a charity that is trying to find a cure for cancer or helps people who have cancer, and tell your grandparents what you're doing.

You could help out at your local house of worship—which might even be the same one your grandparents used to attend—in their name. You might try to start a club with grandchildren of other congregants so that you could share some of the chores. Among the types of assistance that you could provide at a house of worship are cleaning, baby-sitting during services, stuffing envelopes, and ushering.

If you live near a nursing home or a senior center, you could become a volunteer there. Who knows, you might get lucky and meet someone with a grandchild who lives near your grandparents and would be willing to help them.

Also, you might have an elderly neighbor whose grandchildren don't live nearby, or who doesn't have any, and you could do for that person some of the things that you would do for your grandparents.

What's great about helping grandparents is that anything you do, even if it's for someone else, will give them a great deal of pleasure. I know that when they see you and gush over you, telling everybody within hearing distance how great you are, it does embarrass you a little. But don't let that stop you. After all, what if you did a good deed on their behalf and they didn't say anything? So help your grandparents and accept graciously the praise that comes your way.

Now, let's say that your grandparents have always lived near enough so that you've been able to see them regularly, maybe once a week, maybe once a day. That means that ever since you were a little baby, they've been a part of your life. Then one day you learn that they're going to be living far away, either because they're mov-

. . . become a volunteer . . .

ing or because your family is moving. This is sad news, no doubt about it, and you'll have to let yourself be sad in order to get over the feeling. If you try to bottle it up, then the feeling of sadness is likely to surface again later on. But if you let yourself be sad, maybe go to your room and cry for a while, you'll end up feeling better more quickly.

In addition to experiencing those sad feelings, you have to be careful not to let them turn into anger. Sure, you could be angry at your grandparents if, for example, they have decided to retire to another, warmer state, such as Florida or Arizona. But they probably have good reasons, including getting away from the cold, which really bothers their arthritis, or giving up shoveling snow, which could actually be dangerous to their hearts. And whatever their reasons for moving away, they're going to miss you terribly, so it's not something you should hold against them.

If it's your parents who have decided to move away, you shouldn't be mad at them either. Obviously, moving away is going to cause you to miss more than your grandparents—your room, your house, your friends, your school—but again, if you look closely at the situation, I'm sure you'll realize that your parents have good reason for deciding to move. Probably it has something to do with one or both of their jobs. Also, they'll miss many of the same things you will—in particular, your grandparents.

As you know, communicating over long distances is not the same as talking with someone nearby, even if you have every one of the most modern tools of communication. It's not going to come naturally to you. For example, if you've never written a letter to your grandparents, you're going to have to learn how to do it. And when you spoke with them on the phone, which you may have done quite often when they were around the corner, you probably didn't need to say much because you knew you were going to see them in person very soon. Now you'll have to learn how to talk on a long-distance phone call.

And just think how much is communicated to them when they see you in the flesh. Right away they know how tall you are, what kind of clothes you like to wear, how long your hair is, how tanned your skin is, whether you have any cuts or scrapes on your knees, and, by looking into your eyes, maybe even whether you're happy or sad. They're still going to want to know all those things, and the only way they're going to find out is if you tell them, and that's going to be hard, especially at first.

Well, I've shared with you all the ways of maintaining close contact when your grandparents live far away. But before you can employ them, you'll have to learn to think about your faraway grandparents a little more. If you get 100 on a test, say to yourself, I can't wait to write to Grandma about it. If you hit a home run, teach your dog a new trick, reach a glass on a high shelf for the first time, learn to roller-blade—whatever it is, think what you're going to say to Grandma and Grandpa about it, and then it will be easy to reach out to them in any of the ways I've suggested.

5

How to Find a Grandparent

When I was a little girl, my grandmother would often take me to a park in Frankfurt, Germany, where we lived. Some of our other relatives would also go there, and while we children played, the adults would talk. Every time we went, my grandmother would buy me a delicious white pastry called *Baiser mit Schlagsahne*, a light meringue, and the memories of that park are a mixture of sights, sounds, and tastes.

I didn't return to Germany for a long time after I left. But the first time I went back as an adult, I wanted to visit that park. However, I couldn't bear the thought of going without my grandmother. My mother-in-law was staying at a nursing home nearby, but she wasn't well enough to travel. I went to the home anyway, with the intention of "borrowing" a grandmother. I asked one of the other residents to go with me, and I even managed to find the same pastry that I remembered. We both ate some while I talked about my grandmother. I did that several times, taking different women, and I promised myself never to go to that park without a "grandmother."

Since I never saw my grandmother and my other set of grandparents after I was ten years old, I know what it means not to have grandparents. But as you see, I didn't let it stop me entirely from enjoying the benefits of having them. Perhaps you're one of those people who can't spend a lot of time with your grandparents. Maybe they were around at one time, but then either died or moved away. Or maybe they're too sick to see you very often. Since you have two sets, it may be a combination of these factors. Whatever the reason, if you fall into the group of have-nots, then you're missing out on some very important aspects of life. But if you're willing to take some initiative, all is not lost.

While there are many children who do not have available grandparents, there are also many older people who do not have available grandchildren, and they wish they had. Some of these people are grandparents who rarely get to see their grandchildren, while others just don't have any. All of them have the desire to interact with children.

Why would they want to be around children who weren't related to them? Mostly because they are lonely. Maybe they don't have any family members who live close by, or the ones who are around don't have much time for them. Even if they do see family, they probably don't have a job to go to, so they're still left with lots of time on their hands. And even if they visit friends with whom they play cards or go for walks, they have empty hours that need to be filled by something more satisfying than watching television.

"Okay," you ask, "so these older people want to hang out with me, but what do I get out of it? I'd rather be with my friends, and I might even find watching television more interesting." This is a natural reaction.

The answer is that you could have just as much fun with them as you could with your real grandparents, once you break the ice. All the activities that you can do with grandparents you can do with these foster grandparents, once you get comfortable with one another.

I'm sure of this because the people who volunteer to be grandparents are very special. Before you even meet them, you know they like kids. Also, you know that they have the time and the desire to do things with you. And since they *want* to be with you, they'll probably work extra hard at making sure that you have a good time and will want to keep seeing them. They might even try to spoil you a bit.

It's possible that you have specific needs that they could fill. Have you ever heard the term "latchkey child"? It's used to describe children whose parents work and who are alone, without any adult supervision, from the time they get home from school until their parents return. Many of these children feel lonely. They do their homework, but might have a question about it. They make themselves a snack, but would love to have someone there with them while they eat. They do their chores, but could use a little help. They watch TV, but would prefer to have someone they could talk to. If there were a grandparent around, that would be great. But if there isn't, a substitute grandparent would be a wonderful find.

Or what if you play a sport like Little League baseball or go to a dance class? Is it sometimes a problem getting a ride there from your parents? Well, your foster grandparent might be just the person to take you and cheer you on.

Or what if your parents go out at night? Wouldn't it be better to have someone you know and like as a baby-sitter rather than someone you see only occasionally?

And what if you get sick and have to stay home from school? If your parents can't get any time off from work, who will give you your medicine and make you some chicken soup for lunch?

So you see, having a substitute grandparent available and nearby could be a great thing. The problem is finding this unrelated grandparent.

Your first step is to ask your parents. This is not a task that you can handle alone. While most people, especially those of a certain age, are kind and safe, not everyone can be completely trusted. You need the advice of an adult with the experience to judge people.

The first place you should look is in your own backyard, so to speak. There might be an older neighbor who would make a perfect candidate. If your neighborhood doesn't have any suitable people, you might find someone at your place of worship. Or simply ask the people you know, as one of them might have an older relative who lives in the area.

There are programs in which older people volunteer to be foster grandparents. Many are part of a national program called the Foster Grandparents Program. These programs are designed to help children in need, so they are directed mainly at children who are in institutions such as foundling hospitals and orphanages. They are at least partially funded by the federal government and have strict

. . . in your own backyard . . .

guidelines as to which children they can help and which they can't. But if this type of program is not right for you, there may be other organizations in your area that could help you search.

There are several local organizations that might be able to put you in touch with senior citizens who want to be foster grandparents, or at least to provide you and your parents with a pool of senior citizens whom you could contact. Besides houses of worship, these include senior residences; YMCAs or YMHAs; Police Athletic Leagues; ACTION, the Federal Domestic Volunteer Agency; and other governmental and charitable services that deal with seniors.

Once you find someone who is interested, your parents could invite him or her over for a cup of tea and discuss the possibilities. If they think the relationship might work out, the next step would be for you and that person to get to know each other better. Probably you should meet again in your own home and keep it short, just to "break the ice," or get over the initial nervousness that people feel when they meet someone new.

If that meeting goes well, then you could make plans to do something together outside your home, such as attending a ball game or going out for ice cream. At the beginning, you still might be a bit nervous together, but my guess is that after an hour or so you'll both feel as if you've known each other a long time.

For this to happen, you have to be open-minded and give the person a fair chance. If this "grandparent" does one thing that you don't like, don't close your mind to the relationship. Give him or her a second chance and try to make it work. That doesn't mean it will, but if you don't give the relationship a chance to develop, then it definitely won't.

With enough goodwill and patience on your part, plus a dash of good luck, you might gain an important new person in your life, one who can provide many of the advantages that you'd get from a natural grandparent and some that you might not get. For example, on your first few visits, you probably won't take along any brothers or sisters, in order not to overwhelm your foster grandparent. That means there will be peace and quiet at this person's house and you won't have to fight for his or her attention. You can talk quietly, or maybe even concentrate on your homework.

And you won't be the only one who benefits from having a foster grandparent. You can be sure that your parents will appreciate your foster grandparent's driving you to the library or fixing your dinner, things they would otherwise have done. But mostly they'll appreciate—as you will—having your life enriched by this special new relationship.

6

Divorce and Grandparents

If you were asked what is the worst emotional event that can occur in a person's life, I'm sure you could guess that the answer is when a close relative, such as a husband or wife or child, dies. But did you know that the second worst is when someone gets divorced? So if the people getting divorced become very upset at what is happening, obviously their children will also be deeply unhappy. They might even feel worse than the adults.

If your parents have gone through a divorce or are in the process, then probably someone has told you that you should not blame yourself for what has happened to their marriage. I want to repeat this because I know how hard it is for you to really believe it: if your parents get divorced, it is not because of anything you did. Still, just because something is not your fault might not stop you from feeling guilty. You might remember something you did, such as breaking a window while playing ball, that triggered a fight between your parents, and you feel bad about it. That type of incident, or even a hundred others like it, wouldn't cause parents to divorce. But no matter how many times you're told that you're not to blame for the breakup, you probably can't help saying to yourself, There must have been something I could have done to prevent this divorce.

Besides feeling guilty, you're bound to feel depressed that your parents have separated, angry that your family life has been torn apart, and frightened of the future. While these feelings may diminish in time, they won't ever completely go away.

What's important is that you understand the source of those feelings and learn to deal with them so that they don't interfere with your life. If you are having trouble doing that, then you should ask to see a counselor of some sort. It is difficult for an adult to deal with all of these emotions, and many adults seek help, so you shouldn't hesitate to ask for help also.

Unfortunately, professional counseling is not available everywhere or to everyone, so you might not be able to get it. If you can't—and even if you can—you should talk to your grandparents. Just telling them how you feel will make you feel better. Also, they might have some good advice on how to begin the healing process that you need to go through. And if you need to cry, you don't have to be ashamed in front of them. They'll definitely be sympathetic to your tears because they will probably have shed some themselves.

In times like these, don't be afraid of the costs of calling your grandparents if they live far away. I'm sure they'll even accept the charges if you call collect.

. . . talk to your grandparents.

If you can visit your grandparents, so much the better. Their homes make a good refuge when you're feeling angry at your mom and dad for divorcing. Again, it's natural to feel that anger, but since your parents are going through a very hard time, and since you really do love them both, it might be better for you to vent your frustrations on somebody else. If Grandma and Grandpa live close by, go over to their home (call them up if you need a ride). It will do you good to speak with them, and the change of scenery will help you feel better as well.

Sadly, you may not be allowed to see your grandparents, at least not all of them. Sometimes the fighting that goes on between a mother and father grows to such a degree that the parent who has custody of the children—meaning the parent with whom the children live—won't allow the children to see their other parent or any relatives on that side of the family, including grandparents.

To my way of thinking, this is a horrible thing to do to a child. If you love your grandparents and they love you, you should be allowed to see them no matter how bad the differences between your parents. But as I said, divorce causes intense feelings, and when those feelings include bitterness, many people other than your parents can be affected.

It's important for you to know that there's nothing your grandparents can do about this situation, at least not legally. The courts have ruled that in such circumstances, the grandparents do not have a legal right to see their grandchildren. I think it's wrong to discriminate against grandparents in this way, and there are groups of grandparents who are trying to fight it, but for right now, that's the law.

But even if your grandparents' hands are tied, I don't think yours have to be. Try to send a note or make a call to them from time to time. Now, I don't want you to get into trouble, so be careful how you do it, but don't cut your grandparents out of your life. Try to find a way to let them know that you still love them, even if circumstances prevent your seeing them for the time being.

Just because people are your grandparents doesn't make them always right. You may have grandparents who take sides and say something against one of your parents. I want you to ask them to stop the very first time they do it. They're entitled to their opinions, and maybe one of your parents did hurt the other. But your parents are still your parents, and you should not be put in the middle of any such arguments. As a child, you need and deserve protection from what is happening to your parents, and it is your grandparents' first duty to provide you with a safe, calm environment. Certainly they should never vent their own feelings on you.

Holidays are times when divorces are most keenly felt. Whereas before the divorce you might have seen one or both sets of grandparents on Thanksgiving, Hanukkah, or Christmas, now your time is going to be divided in some way, and there's a good chance that you won't be able to see everybody you used to see each year.

On these important days, you have to accept some responsibility for staying in touch. If you can't be with a grandmother whom you used to see every holiday, you have to realize that she's just as sad about it as you are. So make an effort to get in touch with her. Call her if you can, or send a note or card ahead of time if you think you won't be able to call. I'm sure she'll always be happy to know

Call her if you can . . .

that you love her, but holidays are a time when some old people, especially those who don't have a partner, can feel unusually lonely, so hearing from you on the holidays is particularly important.

After a divorce, seeing your grandparents at all may become difficult, more so if you end up living part-time with each parent. What sometimes happens is that because you have to divide your time between your parents, none of it is left for your grandparents. Even if your grandparents live nearby, during the week you may be too busy with homework, sports, and friends to pop over to their house. If on weekends, when you used to visit them, you now go to your other parent's house, then you can see that no time is left for your grandparents. I can't tell you exactly how to fit them in, because I don't know your specific circumstances, but I do know that you'll want to try.

You could find yourself in the reverse situation, suddenly spending a lot more time with some of your grandparents than you ever did before. Let's say that during the week you live with your mom, who had to get a job after the divorce. If you have grandparents nearby, they may be picking you up from school and taking you to their house until dinnertime. Or, if you live with your dad, who goes on the road a lot, you may go to school near your grandparents and live with them during the week. It might even happen that because of the commotion surrounding the divorce, or for some other reason, you end up living with your grandparents full-time. And this certainly will require some adjustment.

Divorce changes families in many different ways. While the initial effect is one of separation and loss, if one or both of your parents remarry, you will find yourself with new family members, such as a stepmother or stepfather. When that happens, you may also inherit some step-grandparents.

While getting along with your stepmother or stepfather might require a lot of work, it should be much easier to deal with step-grandparents. Since they are not as close to the whole process, they could be very much like foster grandparents, willing to act as real grandparents toward you whenever they get the chance. Of course, you might be having trouble finding the time to see your real grandparents, but if these step-grandparents are nearby and come over, maybe to see their real grandchildren, now your stepbrothers and stepsisters, don't turn them away. There's no limit to how many people you can love, and every time you add someone new to that list, you're also adding to the love that you receive.

It's possible that you have step-grandparents who resent you. They may be upset about the divorce, worried that their real grandchildren aren't getting enough attention, and trying to make up for it. If they do act like that—if they bring over lots of presents for their real grandchildren and nothing for you, for example—you're going to feel bad. If this happens, make sure you talk about it with your mother or father. Your step-grandparents probably don't intend to make you feel slighted; they're only trying to make their grandchildren feel better. Let's hope that once they're told that what they're doing is hurting you, they'll be more thoughtful.

Divorce isn't easy on any family member. The new "blended" family that you'll be part of won't ever be a perfect fit. But since you can't do anything about it, you might as well make the best of it. And if one of the results is that you have some new grandparents, then try to accept them as something positive.

7

Older Grandparents

While it is true that grandparents come in many different varieties, none are very young, and a lot are old. There are many advantages to growing old, such as watching your children grow up and then playing with your grandchildren. But there are certainly some problems that accompany old age. Your eyesight might get worse, especially at night. You might lose some of your hearing and need a hearing aid. You might not be able to move around as fast as you once did or pick up heavy packages or bend easily.

As a child, you are young and the various parts of your body are probably working well, so it might be hard for you to imagine what it is like to have a physical disability. To appreciate this better, try simulating a physical impairment of some sort and living with it for a few hours or even an entire day.

For example, you may have noticed that when your grandparents are walking out of your house at night, they seem to be extra careful. To see what that feels like, walk around outside some evening while wearing dark sunglasses. You'll come to realize how difficult it is going down stairs when you can't see where to put your feet. So, if you have some dimly lit steps near your door, be sure to grab a flashlight to help your grandparents reach the street comfortably and safely.

To simulate losing your sense of hearing, try spending an hour or two with a wad of cotton in each ear. Or put on a pair of somebody else's glasses to experience what it's like to have cataracts.

Now use your imagination. Whether or not you've ever broken a bone, imagine what life would be like if you had to wear a cast on your leg. You wouldn't be able to run. Going up and down stairs would be difficult. You might even be uncomfortable when sitting down or trying to sleep. Having to put up with all this would probably make you a little crabby at times. Maybe you'd see your little brother running around and you'd snap at him for making so much noise, not because the noise bothered you but because you were jealous that you couldn't run around with him. Try to feel that grumpiness, and you'll understand why older people can be quick to get angry—often it comes from the frustration they feel at not being able to do all the things they used to do.

Some sicknesses, like colds, last only a short time, and most likely those are the ones you're used to having. But old people may develop ailments that will never go away. Maybe they'll always have to use a cane, or a wheelchair. This is part of life for many people, and if it isn't yet for any of your grandparents, you should be aware that it still might be.

If their health does start to fail, you are certainly going to want them to feel better, and you'll try to help. You might get them a cup of tea or massage their aching muscles. But your main job will be to cheer them up. Many studies have shown that a person's mental state has an effect on his or her physical health. They've found that positive thoughts can make a sick person feel better, while negative moods may worsen health problems. So you see, by picking up the spirits of a grandparent who is ill, or anybody for that matter, you can play a very important role in helping that person recover.

What else can you do? Older people often need help with chores that require bending, such as gardening or loading the dishwasher, or with those that take a lot of strength, such as shoveling snow or vacuuming the house. By lending them your young bones and muscles, you can really make their lives a lot easier. You see, even if your grandparents can afford to hire help, at least to shovel the walk, they may prefer not to have strangers around, so they do these chores themselves and risk injury. When you pitch in, then, you're really doing them a great service. And I do mean pitch in. If you offer help in a casual way, your grandparents may not admit to needing it. You have to go over to their house, do whatever needs to be done, and not take no for an answer.

Obviously, the closer your grandparents live to you, the easier this will be to do. But even if they don't live nearby, you can still help when you see them. Ask your parents to leave enough time for you to do some chores for them. If you go to their home for dinner, get there two hours early and start right in doing whatever you can.

Let's say that your grandparents live too far away to visit regularly. You can still find ways of helping them. For example, if you mow lawns in your area, you could set aside the money you get from one of your customers to hire a kid in your grandparents' neighborhood to mow their lawn. It would be even better if you could find a kid who lives near your grandparents, with grandparents who live near you. It wouldn't be easy, but you could try. If you're really industrious, you could start a bulletin board on a computer network, asking for kids with whom you could swap grandparents.

Besides physical assistance, your grandparents can certainly use your moral support. Older people, particularly if they have retired, can have too much free time on their hands. Of course, if they still play golf or tennis or knit or do whatever it is they enjoy, that's fabulous. But if they're no longer able to do the things they want, then they might spend that free time feeling sad. So what's the best thing you can do? Share some of that free time with them.

"But what can I do with such elderly people?" you might ask.

Well, if you've got ten board games at your house and they have none, just show up at their door with Parcheesi under one arm and chess under the other, and you can spend an entertaining afternoon together. If there's a model airplane that you've been meaning to build, have your grandfather help you, even if all he does is find the next piece for you. You could start a quilt with your grandmother. You could take over some paints or felt-tip markers and make pictures together. You could do crossword puzzles together. You could rent a movie you think they would like. Comedies are good to see with other people because laughter is contagious. If your grandparents speak another language, have them give you lessons. If they've got a piano and you play, give them a concert.

. . . *spend an entertaining afternoon together.*

It doesn't matter what you do, it only matters that you go to your grandparents' home prepared to do something that will make them feel better. Remember what I said earlier: inside each of your grandparents there's still that little boy or girl. Your grandma may not be able to jump rope anymore, but she'd like to, and your grandpa may not be able to play catch with you, but there is nothing that would please him more.

On second thought, with your help maybe your grandparents *can* do these things—at least to some degree. For example, tie one end of a rope to a piece of furniture and give your grandmother the other end, then let her turn it while you jump. Work as a team and count how many times you can jump while she turns the rope. And if your grandpa can't throw the ball, maybe he can roll it to you across a table. Even if you don't do it for long, it will give him a lot of pleasure.

This reminds me of a story my friend Peter told me. Peter was fourteen, and his grandfather was eighty-two. The grandfather had trouble getting around because of a bad back, so about the only thing Peter could do with him was play board games. Since these games take a long time, Peter didn't know what to do when he had only half an hour to spend with his grandpa.

One day they were sitting at the breakfast table, and Peter took a quarter out of his pocket and started spinning it on the table. He was trying to see how long he could make it spin. His grandfather then took a quarter out of his pocket and did the same. Then his sister, Gabrielle, hearing the noise, joined them and asked her grandfather if she could have a quarter. It was a simple game, seeing whose coin would spin the longest, but they all had a good time, laughing out loud when the coins bumped each other or fell off the table. After that, Peter, Gabrielle, and their grandpa played this game during almost every visit, and it really made the time fly.

What if you have grandparents who've grown so old that their faculties have faded dramatically and they're in a hospital or nursing home, barely able to lift their head from the pillow. Does that leave you without any options? Of course not. In the first place, if you visit them with other people, such as one of your parents or a sibling or a cousin, and just have a conversation around them, that will make them feel better. But if you can't do that, then bring a good book and read out loud to them. It's your presence and the sound of your voice that are important, not what you do.

8

When a Grandparent Dies

Because grandparents are among the oldest people you know, there's a good chance that the first important member of your family to die will be a grandparent. Certainly some of you have already dealt with, or may first have to deal with, the death of someone close to you who is not a grandparent, be it a parent, brother, sister, aunt, uncle, or dear friend. And I know that even the death of a pet can cause a lot of pain.

No matter how many times it happens, no one ever gets used to losing loved ones. Of course, depending on the person lost, you will have different emotions each time. If a grandfather whom you rarely saw died, you might feel guilty for not having spent more time with him, though you might not feel his loss heavily, because he didn't play an important role in your everyday life. However, if you saw your grandfather every day before he died, then you would miss him an awful lot.

Sometimes people try to block out the hurt feelings they have when someone has died. They find it easier to keep from thinking this person has died than to face the pain that overcomes them when the death does come to mind. Males, especially, try to bury their feelings because they don't want to cry, which they feel makes them look like "sissies." But there are whole cultures that do not believe in showing emotion. In Germany, where I was born, crying is looked down upon, and in England men are often told to "keep a stiff upper lip," meaning not to cry.

In my opinion, there's some good in that and some bad. I certainly understand your need for privacy, that you might not want to go around crying or looking sad in public. But if you force that emotion down too deep, then you won't be able to mourn properly, and that's not good for you. Mourning is the natural process that allows you to accept the loss of a loved one. You may mourn for a long time or a short time, depending on how close you felt to the person who passed away, but whatever the period, you do need to mourn.

What happens if you don't mourn? The hurt that you feel remains stuck inside you, where it can actually cause damage. If each time someone you love dies—and this is bound to happen many times during a lifetime—you bury your sadness, you're going to end up burying all the rest of your emotions, too. Eventually you're going to have trouble feeling much of anything, including emotions like love and compassion. You could wind up a cold and lonely person.

So you see, mourning is a natural, positive way for you to come to terms with the death of someone you love. Now, as I said, you don't have to mourn in public. You don't have to break down and cry in front of your friends or your family or anyone else if it makes you feel uncomfortable. Mourning is not any more effective because you do it in public. You can mourn all by yourself, under your covers in the dark at night, if you want. If you've ever gone to a funeral, you may have noticed that there are some people who are crying and many who are not, including those who were close to the person who died. But don't assume that the people who are not crying in public haven't done so in private.

There are no hard-and-fast rules about mourning. All it really means is that you allow yourself to feel the emotion that surfaces when you think of the person who has died. You will feel sad enough to want to cry if you really felt close to the deceased. But when you remember that person, you will also think of the happy times you shared—the times you laughed together, felt good about something you did together, touched each other in some way.

At first, when you recall those happy moments, you may feel sad because you will not be able to experience any more such moments with that person. This may even make you cry. But over time, and no one can say exactly how long it will take, you'll be able to think about the person who has died without crying. Recalling the good times you had together will bring a warm feeling to your heart instead of an empty feeling to the pit of your stomach.

People who don't mourn usually don't make this progress. Because they are afraid of letting go, afraid of their own emotions, they bottle them up. How do they do that? By not allowing themselves to think about the dead person. But while they may feel that they've conquered their emotions by stifling them, actually the re-

. . . remember that person . . .

verse has happened and they will never be able to have those warm, happy thoughts about the person who has died. In the long run, they will have lost more than they have gained, even though they might not realize it at the time.

Some people develop a problem with mourning: they struggle so hard to keep themselves from crying in public that they can't let their feelings out in private. What should you do if this happens to you? I suggest using a prop, something that will help trigger those tears. It could be a picture of your grandfather. You could take it into your room, lock the door, and look at it while thinking of him. This might be enough to help you open yourself up to those feelings.

If that doesn't work, try renting a sad movie. There are many good tearjerkers, and if you watch one of those, the tears might start to fall. Anyone who sees you crying probably will be crying, too, because of the movie, and you'll be able to safeguard your privacy. Now, it's certainly all right if people, especially family members, see you cry about the death of your grandfather. But I understand why you might not want to be seen crying. Your parents might make too big a fuss over it, or an older brother or sister might tease you. So if you have to use the movie as an excuse, go right ahead.

As sad as it is to lose a grandfather, or anyone you love, the saddest thing is to force yourself to forget about him just because you don't want to deal with the initial feeling of loss. It's sad for you because you'll miss out on the joy that all those memories can bring, and it's sad for him because he's forgotten by one of his grandchildren. So be brave and face up to the initial pain that his death causes you. The sooner you do, the sooner you'll be able to recover some of your loss, the fond memories of the times you spent together.

9

Grandparents and Computers

As people get older, they reach many of the goals they set for themselves when they were younger. They've finished raising their children, and however the children have turned out, there's not much more they can do. These older people may have stopped going to work, and with many big companies forcing their employees to take early retirement, that time may have arrived before they really wanted it to. The future suddenly has become today, and without any new goals, they find growing older very bleak.

What senior citizens need are new objectives so that they can look to the future rather than at the past. Not only is learning how to use a computer a very good goal to have, but computers themselves open up whole new worlds to conquer because every program becomes a challenge.

Although you can find me listed on the Internet and there's a CD-ROM version of a book I wrote, I have to admit that I am computer-illiterate. I don't even know how to turn a computer on, much less sit down and work with it. Part of the reason for this is that I grew up before learning to type was a requirement in school, and if you have to hunt and peck at the keys on a keyboard, the computer itself isn't going to help you work any faster.

I am not alone among my peers in being computer-illiterate. But I also know that many senior citizens regularly use a computer— about 20 percent of people sixty-five to sixty-nine years old own one—so this is not a skill that's beyond our ability, merely one that most of us don't find necessary.

Another reason why many older people shy away from computers is that they don't know where to learn about them. They don't feel comfortable taking a course, and they're scared away by the big computer books.

Can you guess why I've brought up this topic? That's right, I would like you to share your computer skills with your grandparents. Don't be surprised by their initial resistance. After all, if they've managed to live their entire lives without the benefit of computers, they're likely to say, "Why should I start now?" And if, like me, they're not good at typing and think a mouse belongs only in a trap, they're also going to be a little afraid of looking bad when they do sit down in front of one of those machines.

Now, if your grandparents are still working, and doing a thousand other things, then when they say they don't have time, they probably have a legitimate excuse. They may not need a new field to conquer. But if they have free time on their hands, especially if

. . . share your computer skills . . .

they've retired, then I think that you should put as much effort as you can into changing their attitudes about computers.

Your first job is to introduce your grandparents to the programs that will interest them. If they hate card games, then it certainly won't help to show them that they can play solitaire or poker on the computer. On the other hand, if they travel a lot, showing them how easy it is to print out a map of any city in the United States or in the world might intrigue them.

What I think would attract them most is the way computers can make communicating easier. If your grandparents have family scattered all over, then explaining to them how easy and inexpensive it would be to send letters to everyone via E-mail might get them hooked. And you can play an important role in getting them started.

For their first E-mail, have them dictate to you, so that you do the typing. Then show them that you can send the letter to anyone else who has a computer with a modem. They'll be amazed, they'll praise you to the heavens for being so smart—and they'll also see that it's not really all that complicated.

Some other ways in which they can use a computer, depending on their interests, include: getting stock quotes and even buying and selling stocks by computer; banking by computer, checking balances anytime they want on their computer screen and paying bills; and shopping by computer. There are even programs that make it a cinch to put together a family tree. And if you have a single grandparent living alone, then he or she can chat with other people who share similar interests over a chat line, or just enjoy reading messages that other people post.

Be sure to tell your grandparents that they are not alone, that there are special services aimed at senior citizens. One forum, called Seniornet, which is available through America Online, can not only put your grandparents in touch with other seniors but also help them get all sorts of interesting information that might be of use to them. The available topics include health issues, computer problems, and services for seniors. Two groups providing this information are the Social Security Administration and the Gray Panthers. Another forum, called Seniorcom (which can be found on the World Wide Web at http://www.senior.com), offers news, information about senior issues, and advertising messages from lawyers, insurance companies, and cruise lines.

Now, will your lessons get your grandparents interested enough to buy their own computer? Maybe, if you can show them that it will bring you closer together. You would really have to commit yourself to sending them E-mail letters, and maybe get your siblings and cousins to do the same. If they're convinced that having a computer would keep them in closer touch with their family, and if it's within their financial means, I think they'll buy one.

By the way, in addition to sharing your computer skills, you can also help your grandparents with electronic equipment that they might already have. Many adults have no idea how to program their VCRs to tape a television show, and some, like me, have trouble playing a tape. I'm sure that VCRs are old hat to you and that you could program them in your sleep. So make a point of going over to your grandparents' house and seeing if they need some help with their video machine. They might not want to bother you, but if you offer, I'm sure they'll take you up on it. After you've shown them what to do, it would be great if you wrote out everything in big letters and put the paper near the VCR. That way they'll be able to refresh their memories after you've left.

Another wonderful gadget that can be confusing is the TV remote control. These days remotes have so many buttons, and the print on them is so small, that they can be difficult to use. Even if your grandparents know the basic operations, there might be other tricks their TVs can do that they don't know about. Spend some time with their remote, figuring out all of its capabilities, and then show them. As with the VCR, leave them a set of written instructions. If they have a lot of remote controls and get confused about which is which, maybe you could get your parents to buy them one of the universal remotes, then program it to control all of their machines and really simplify their lives.

Telephones can also be baffling. Oh, I'm sure your grandparents know how to dial a number, but if their phone has speed-dialing capabilities, have they programmed into it the numbers they dial frequently? There's a chance that they haven't, and it's something you could do for them. And if they have an answering machine, find out if they know how to use all of its features. Again, you might be able to simplify their lives by teaching them, for example, how to retrieve messages from outside their home.

I know that I still have trouble using a telephone credit card. If your grandparents do, too, you could read up on its applications and give them some lessons. Now, since you know that I'm a grandparent, you may be wondering why my grandson hasn't done all of this for me. The answer is simple—he's only six. And my granddaughter is only one.

I don't know exactly why it is that young people are so much

Spend some time with their remote . . .

better at using this equipment than we older folk. One reason must be that it's always been around you. Also, learning new things is easier when you're very young. And peer pressure probably has something to do with it. If all your friends are playing with computers, then you have the incentive to learn, too. But if none of your grandparents' friends is computer-literate, and especially if their friends make fun of your grandparents for trying, they're going to be less willing to leap into cyberspace.

Here's where you come in. Isn't it wonderful that you have such an influence on your grandparents? It used to be thought that children should be seen and not heard. That was because children couldn't teach their elders very much of anything, since they really didn't know anything that adults didn't. Now things have changed, and more and more adults are willing to learn from their children and grandchildren.

Why is this good for you? Well, one of the best ways to learn is to teach. You may be using your computer every day, but when you sit down and try to explain to somebody else what to do, and that person starts asking questions, you suddenly realize that there are some things about your computer that you don't know very well, and so you study them in order to be able to pass on the information. That's what your teachers do. Even if they've taught a course a hundred times, each year they learn something new because their students ask them questions. So by teaching your grandparents, or even your parents, about computers, you'll become more knowledgeable. And I believe you'll also become more appreciative of what a teacher does, which will make you a better student.

Finally, teaching your grandparents how to use a computer will bring you closer together. If your grandfather taught you the rules of baseball, then you'll have something in common with him whenever you watch a game. Even after you've become a grown-up and he's passed away, you'll still think of him every time you go out to the ballpark. The same thing will happen if you teach him about computers. Every time each of you flicks on your machine, you'll think of each other, and those warm thoughts are worth more than anything else in the world.

Afterword

One day, when I was about four or five years old, I was visiting my grandparents' farm. My mother's parents lived in a small village. I was a city child, and I decided that it was unfair to have all the geese locked up in a pen. I thought they should be allowed to run free, so I opened the gate and shooed them out. The geese scattered all over the village, and it took my grandparents, along with their neighbors, almost all day to round them up.

Now, if this farm had belonged to my parents, I would have been punished. But because it was my grandparents' farm and I was their only grandchild, I don't even remember being yelled at.

That's just the way grandparents are. As people get older and approach the end of their days, they begin to appreciate life in a new way. Something that once might have seemed very serious to them,

like rounding up dozens of geese, loses its importance when compared to the joys of having a granddaughter. Instead of looking at
a grandchild only as a separate entity, grandparents think of their
own passing and see in that grandchild a continuation of their
lives. Naturally, the more they see themselves in the child, the more
indulgent and forgiving they become.

One of the wonderful aspects of the grandparent/grandchild relationship is that both have so much to gain from it. You, as a
grandchild, receive a ton of love and endless emotional support. You
develop a more positive outlook toward older people, realizing that
they are not all alike. And you learn not to fear old age as much as
you might if you were never around older people.

Your grandparents experience the joy of holding a newborn
baby again, followed by all the other delights of being around children, without having to bear the full responsibility for their care.
Grandchildren give them something to look forward to, as well as
the knowledge that they will leave behind something of real sig-
nificance.

The roles of grandchild and grandparent have gone through
some significant changes over the years, and continue to evolve as
our society develops in new ways. Grandparents certainly want to
maintain close family relations, but they are also building new, independent lives for themselves, apart from their children and grandchildren, in ways that were once unimaginable. Remember, when
people began migrating from Europe to America, for the most part
it was the young ones who left and the older people who stayed
behind. Now it's the senior set who are packing their bags and head-
ing for new horizons.

. . . the more indulgent and forgiving they become.

The practice of grandparents leaving their families behind to retire in special communities is still so recent that I wonder if it will
continue. Even the idea of retirement is relatively new, as most people used to work until they either became too sick or just dropped
dead. They may have slowed down and done less, but they didn't
turn off their work lives like a light switch.

But grandchildren have also changed. They are no longer dependent on their grandparents and so have a much more casual at-
titude toward them. They don't visit their grandparents because they
have to but because they want to. And they're not content to be seen
and not heard; they want to have an active relationship with their
grandparents.

And these changes have not run their course or finished mold-
ing our lives. What the relationship between grandparents and
grandchildren will be in the future we can only guess. It may be
that our society is paying too high a price to have grandparents and
their families live so far apart. Although I doubt that we will ever
again live under one roof in one giant room, it wouldn't surprise
me if someday soon families stopped drifting apart and started
moving closer together.

While in the United States we celebrate Grandparents Day, in
Japan people celebrate Revere Your Elders Day, on which all older
people are honored for their lifelong accomplishments. Because of
the way they're treated, older people in Japan look at each new
birthday not with dread but with pride.

If there is one hope that I have for you, it is that you won't ever
take your grandparents for granted. I have tried to make you see
your grandparents in ways that may never have occurred to you,

and I would like you to use those insights to build a new relation-ship with all of your grandparents—those you see all the time, those you see only once in a while, and those whom you will never see again. Because whether your grandparents are in the next room or the next life, they will always be your grandparents and will always influence your life, through the genes they've passed on and through the family ties they've made. They are an important part of your life, and the more you develop your relationship with them, the more developed you will be as a human being.